Selected Poems of Yone Noguchi

Selected Poems of Yone Noguchi

Yone Noguchi

MINT EDITIONS

Selected Poems of Yone Noguchi was first published in 1921.

This edition published by Mint Editions 2021.

ISBN 9781513282527 | E-ISBN 9781513287546

Published by Mint Editions®

MINT EDITIONS

minteditionbooks.com

Publishing Director: Jennifer Newens
Design & Production: Rachel Lopez Metzger
Project Manager: Micaela Clark
Typesetting: Westchester Publishing Services

In Memory of Basho, a Hokku Poet
of the Seventeenth Century

Contents

Foreword

I often wonder at the difference between the words of English Poets and the daily speech of common people; and I think that it is not necessary to go to Milton or Dryden for the proof. The poetical words used by Tennyson, Browning, Francis Thompson, and even Yeats, are certainly different from those spoken in the London streets or an English village shadowed by a church spire or darkened by dense foliage. But, on the other hand, how similar are the words of Japanese poets and those of the common people! Is it that the Japanese poets, whether they be Uta poets or Hokku writers, are condescending to the common people? Or is it that the common people of Japan are entering into the realm of poesy? Or is it that our Japanese phraseology belongs to either of them, or does not belong to either of them, through its virtue of being neutral in nature?

Suppose a pensive young lady is standing by a veranda opened to the garden with blooming cherry trees, and her eyes are following the snow-white petals of cherry blossoms hastening to the ground. And suppose she murmurs with a sigh, "Why do the flowers fall in such a flurry?" Now compare such an exclamation with the following Uta poem by Ki no Tomonori:

> "'Tis the spring day
> With lovely far-away light. . .
> Why must the flowers fall
> With hearts unquiet?"

It is plain to see how the words of Japanese poets and common people join hands. This particular point is most worthy of notice in the discussion of the differences and similarities between the East and West in literature.

It is said in the West that the poets are a race apart. The fact that our Japanese poets are not a race apart should be the very focus for a discussion of Japanese poets. While in the West the poets claim special regard and, indeed, immortality for themselves, we in Japan treat the poet as a natural phenomenon, as natural as a flower or bird.

I admit that we Japanese as poets are lacking in creative power, and do not aim, like many Western poets, at becoming rebuilders of life. We are taught not to deal with poetry as a mere art, but to look upon it as the most necessary principle along which our real life shall be developed. When we kneel before poetry, it is our desire to create a clarified pure realm where we can, through the inspiration of rhythm, arrange our own minds. And then we recognise the existence of the compromising ground of passion, where we as members of society find our safety. What great uncompromising creators of passion were Shelley, Byron, Browning, and Swinburne! They were so earnest in their desire for the recreation of life, and not afraid were they, when their desire reached its climax, even to risk reaching a condition of confused intricacy. They were indeed great and wonderful heroes. We cannot help thinking, on the other hand, what cowards the majority of Japanese poets have been.

I respect that attitude of Western poets in wishing to rebuild or recreate their own lives; and also I can well understand why they ascribe importance to their intellectual power. A great literary danger lies in this, of course, because there is nothing more sad and terrible for poets than to enslave themselves to intellect.

But we have also our own literary danger. I mean that we often mistake a simple and cold morality for an art. I should like to know what is a more dangerous thing for poets than this sad morality. There are only a few Japanese poets who have failed from their abuse of moods and passions; but we know so many cases wherein their poetical failure was quite complete under the stifling breath of conventional morality. This damage would not necessarily be below that inflicted by intellect; it might be greater. We notice that the Western poets often attempt to discover a poetical theory even in the waving plaits of Apollo's robe and analyse intellectually a little cloud flying in the sky. Admitting that their poetical theory and intellectual power are doubtless great, I have no hesitation in declaring that it is they who harden, shrink, and wither their own art. It is true to say that they owe much to the matter of form for the great development of their epics and dramas. Also it is true that the undeveloped form of Japanese poetry has given a mighty freedom for our poets to fly into an invisible spiritual domain. We can say again that, if these poets both of the West and the East often stray into the field of non-poetry, it is the result of their too close attachment to forms.

Of course we want more passion and intellect in our Japanese poets, and also properly tempered patience and effort. And at the same time we should hope that the Western poets would forget their passion and intellect to advantage and enter into the real poetical life born out of awakening from madness. I have no quarrel with a critic when he applies the word "mad" to his Western poets; but we Japanese would be pleased to see and admire the rare moment when madness grows strangely calm and returns to its normal condition, and there we will find our own real poetry. Not the moving dynamic aspect of all the phenomena, but their settled still aspect inspired the Japanese poets— at least the Japanese poets of olden days—to real poetry. But I know that the times are changing when we must, I think, cultivate the really living dynamic life. And I am afraid, with many others, that such a new literary step may bring us into an unhappy compromise with Western literature. Of course there are poets and writers both of the East and West who know only how to compromise. But, on the other hand, we have a natural-born Easterner, for instance, Wordsworth, in the West, and there may be a natural-born Westerner in the East, who will bring the East and West together into true understanding, not through faint-hearted compromise but by the real strength of independence which alone knows the meaning of harmony.

To-day we must readjust the meanings of all things or give a new interpretation to all the old meanings; and we must solve the problem of life and the world from our real obedience to laws and knowledge that will make the inevitable turn to a living song, and learn the true meaning of time from the evanescence of psychical life; then our human lives will become true and living.

We must realise the ephemeral aspect of moments when time moves, and also the still aspect of infinity when it settles down; seek the meaning of moments out of the bosom of infinity, and again that of infinity from the changing heart of moments—that is the secret of real poetry. The moments that suggest the still aspect of infinity are accidental, therefore living; again the infinity that is nothing but another revelation of moments is absolute, therefore quiet and full of strength and truth. The real poetry should be accidental and also absolute. See the river and trees, see the smiling garden flowers, see the breaking clouds of the sky. See also the lonely moon walking a precipitate pathless way through the clouds. The natural phenomena are, under any circumstances, revealing both meanings of the accidentalism which is born from the absolute. When our great poets of Japan write only of a shiver of a tree or a flower, of a single isolated aspect of nature, that means that they are singing of infinity from its accidental revelation.

The poetical attitude of Wordsworth was anarchical when, singing of the small celandine, daisy, and daffodils, he gave even a little natural phenomenon a great sense of dignity by making it a center of the universe, and broke the stupid sense of proportion by looking on things without discrimination; he was pantheistic, like nearly all Japanese poets and painters, because he was never troubled by any intellectual differentiation, and his clear and guileless eyes went straight into the simplicity that joined the universe and himself into one. His poetical sensibility was very true and plain, and he gained a real sense of the depth of space, the amplitude of time, and the circle of the universal law, and made his life's exigency a new turn of rhythm. I am glad to think of Wordsworth as the first Easterner of English literature.

I do not know what one critic means when he calls Robert Bridges the father of the new poetry, unless he means that Bridges has regained the artless bent of the poetical mind which was lost under the physical vulgarisation of the Mid-Victorian age, and that he has opened his honest eyes upon nature and life. He, like our Japanese Uta or Hokku poets, gazes on life's essential aspects. If the Japanese poets teach the Western poets anything, it is how to return to the most important feature of poetry after clearing away all the débris of literature; their expression is simple, therefore mysterious in many respects; as it is mysterious, it is vivid and fresh. There is nothing more wonderful than the phrase "Seeing poetry exactly;" nobody who has never lived in poetry fully, claims to see its exact existence. And you cannot be taught how to live in it by reason or argument; you must have a sense of adoration that comes only from poetical concentration.

The time is coming when, as with international politics where the understanding of the East with the West is already an unmistakable fact, the poetries of these two different worlds will approach of one another and exchange their cordial greetings. If I am not mistaken, the writers of free verse of the West will be ambassadors to us.

My acknowledgments are due to the editor of the Outlook, New York, for permission to reprint this essay which has appeared in his pages.

YONE NOGUCHI

FROM "SEEN AND UNSEEN" (1897)

What about my Songs

The known-unknown-bottomed gossamer waves of the field are
    coloured by the travelling shadows of the lonely, orphaned
    meadow lark:
At shadeless noon, sunful-eyed,—the crazy, one-inch butterfly
    (dethroned angel?) roams about, her embodied shadow on the
    secret-chattering hay-tops, in the sabre-light.
The Universe, too, has somewhere its shadow;—but what about
    my songs?
An there be no shadow, no echoing to the end,—my broken-throated
    flute will never again be made whole!

Where is the Poet

The inky-garmented, truth-dead Cloud—woven by dumb ghost alone
in the darkness of phantasmal mountain-mouth—kidnapped the
maiden Moon, silence-faced, love-mannered, mirroring her golden
breast in silvery rivulets:

The Wind, her lover, grey-haired in one moment, crazes around the
Universe, hunting her dewy love-letters, strewn secretly upon the
oat-carpets of the open field.

O, drama! never performed, never gossiped, never rhymed! Behold—
to the blind beast, ever tearless, iron-hearted, the Heaven has no
mouth to interpret these tidings!

Ah, where is the man who lives out of himself?—the poet inspired
often to chronicle these things?

The Desert of "No More"

Until Nothing muffles over the Universe of No More, my soul lives
    with the god, darkness and silence.
Ah, great Nothing?
Ah, the all-powerful Desert of No More!—where myriads of beings
    sleep in their eternal death; where the god dies, my soul dies,
    darkness dies, silence dies; where nothing lives, but the Nothing
    that lives to the End.
Listen to the cough of Nature!
After the cough, the Universe is silent again, my soul kissing the ever
    nameless idol faces of the Universe, as in a holy heathen temple.

Seas of Loneliness

Underneath the void-coloured shade of the trees, my "self" passed as a
   drowsy cloud into Somewhere.
I see my soul floating upon the face of the deep, nay the faceless face
   of the deepless deep—
Ah, the Seas of Loneliness!
The mute-waving silence-waters, ever shoreless, bottomless heavenless,
   colourless, have no shadow of my passing soul.
Alas, I, without wisdom, without foolishness, without goodness,
   without badness,—am like God, a negative god at least!
Is that a quail? One voice out of the back-hill jumped into the ocean
   of loneliness.
Alas, what sound resounds; what colour returns; the bottom, the
   heaven, too, reappears!
There is no place of muteness! Yea, my paradise is lost in this moment!
I want not pleasure, sadness, love, hatred, success, unsuccess, beauty,
   ugliness—only the mighty Nothing in No More.

The Garden of Truth

Untimely frosts wreathe over the garden—the staid bottom were air
    the sea.

Alas! from her honeyed rim, frosts steal down like love-messengers
    from the Lady Moon.

A light-walled corridor in Truth's palace; a humanity-guarded chapel
    of God, where brave divinities kneel, small as mice, against the
    shoreless heavens,—the midnight garden, where my naked soul
    roams alone, under the guidance of Silence.

The God-beloved man welcomes, respects as an honoured guest, his
    own soul and body, in his solitude.

Lo! the roses under the night dress themselves in silence, and expect
    no mortal applaud,—content with that of their voiceless God.

LIKE A PAPER LANTERN

"Oh, my friend, thou wilt not come back to me this night!"
I am lonely in this lonely cabin, alas, in the friendless Universe, and
the snail at my door hides stealishly his horns.
"Oh, for my sake, put forth thy honourable horns!"
To the Eastward, to the Westward? Alas, where is Truthfulness?—
Goodness?—Light?
The world enveils me; my body itself this night enveils my soul.
Alas, my soul is like a paper lantern, its pastes wetted off under the
rainy night, in the rainy world.

FROM "THE VOICE OF THE VALLEY" (1898)

I Hail myself as I do Homer

The heart of God, the unpretending heaven, concealing the midnight
    stars in glassing the day of earth,
Showers his brooding love upon the green-crowned goddess, May
    Earth, in heart-lulling mirth.
O Poet, begin thy flight by singing of the hidden soul in vaporous
    harmony;
Startle the lazy noon drowsing in the full-flowing tide of the
    sunbeams nailing thy chants in Eternity!
The melody breathing peace in the name of Spring, calms tear to smile,
    envy to rest.
Ah thou, world of this day, sigh not of the poets who have deserted
    thee—aye, I hail myself as I do Homer!
Behold, a baby flower hymns the creation of the universe in the breeze,
    charming my soul as the lover-moon!
O Yone,—a ripple of the vanity-water, a rain drop from the
    vanity-cloud,—lay thy body under the sun-enamelled shade of
    the trees,
As a heathen idol in an untrodden path awakening in spirit sent by the
    unseen genius of the sphere!
The earth, a single-roomed hermitage for mortals, shows not, unto me
    a door to Death on the joy-carpeted floor—
Aye, I call the once dead light of day from the dark-breasted slumber
    of night!—
I repose in the harmonious difference of the divine Sister and
    Brother,—Voice and Silence in Time.
O Yone, return to Nature in the woodland,—thy home, where
    Wisdom and Laughter entwine their arms!
Ah Cities, scorning the order of the world, ye plunder rest from night,
    paint day with snowy vice,—
Alas, the smoke-dragon obscures the light of God; the sky measuring
    steeple speaks of discontent unto the Heaven!
O Yone, wander not city-ward—there thou art sentenced to veil thy
    tears with smiles!
Behold, the cloud hides the sins of the cities—regiments of
    redwood-giants guard the holy gates of the woodland against
    the shames!

Chant of Nature, O Yone,—sing thy destiny—hymn of darkness for the ivory-browed dawn—
Behold, the deathless Deity blesses thee in silence from the thousand temples of the stars above!

The Night Reverie in the Forest

"Buy my tears that I sucked from the breast of Truth—tears, sister
spirits of Heaven's smile!" sobs the Wind.

Thou pale Wind, tear-vender of the hideous night, no one welcomes
thee with thy unsold tears!

Thou Gipsy-Wind, my fellow-wanderer who fears light, cease thy
plaintive strain of the sweet home ever lost!

"O Poet, sole midnight comforter, share my tears in thy heart ever
tenanted by Autumn!"

Kiss me, Wind, to whom the gates of Spring never swing open, let us
sleep under the weeping candle-star!

O Repose, whose bosom harbours the heavenly dream-ships, welcome
me, an exiled soul!

Thou Forest, where Peace and Liberty divide their wealth with even a
homeless convict.

Let me sleep in thy arm-boughs, safer far than a king's iron castle
guarded by mortal power!

Lull thy guest to reverie, master-spirit of the forest, with thy solemn
love tales of ancient gods!

Here Ease and Grandeur lodge in the forest's heart, where Time ever
reveals his changeless youth.

Five miles I travelled—the black-robed bird-monk had ended his last
prayer, a good-night hymn;

Ten miles,—I lost the home window-light that bids Sorrow and Tears
depart like masterless dogs;

Twenty miles,—the eloping mother-moon had abandoned her child,
my lonely soul.

Thou Darkness, bewailing thy desertion by Light, I deplore my like
fate, echoing thy saddest strain!—

Friend Night, my tears overflow from the love-fountain unto the
sorrow-made dells!

I, an idle singer, fleeing from the world's shame, make a pilgrimage to
an unknown land—O Heaven—or Hell?

Thou Silence, who never responds to mortal's voice, where is the secret
door of Paradise?—Speak once unto me!

O Star, thou radiant spirit of the blessed Beatrice who once guided a
mortal unto Heaven, brighten now my darksome path!

I, a lone pilgrim, knock at the gate of Heaven—nay, the silent castle of
   Repose—O Repose!

Rhyme on, Lady-Rivulet from thy mountain Memnon, thy tunable
   song awakening mortals' vanity-dreams!

Ah, Nakedness! Nakedness—to whom Shame and Pride are buried in
   the peaceful tomb of Faith!

Ah, Loneliness! Loneliness—to whom a boatman of God is the sole
   saviour on the vast Sea of Eternty i!

I repose under the forest's arm-bough—if I awaken not forever, pray,
   brother mortal,

Make my grave under the greenest grass and carve this line *"Here sleeps
   a nameless Poet."*

Song of Day in Yosemite Valley

O thunderous opening of the unseen gate of solemn Heaven's Eternal
 Court!
Behold, clouds, tenants of the sky, sweep down from the Heavens
 unto a secret palace under the Earth!—
Aye, mighty Yosemite!—a glorious troop of the unsuffering souls of gods
Marches on with battle-sound against the unknown castle of Hell!—
Aye, a divine message of Heaven unto Earth—the darksome house of
 mortals—to awake!
Hark—the heart-broken cry of a great Soul!—
Nay, the tempestuous song of Heaven's organ throbbing wild peace
 through the sky and land!
The Shout of Hell wedded to the Silence of Heaven completes the
 Valley concert, forms the true symphony—
The Female-light kissing the breast of the Male-shadow chants the
 sacred Union!
I, a muse from the Orient, where is revealed the light of dawn,
Harken to the welcome strains of genii from the heart of the great
 Sierras—
I repose under the forest-boughs that invoke the Deity's hymn from
 the Nothing-air.
Here, brother mortal, lies the path like Beauty's arm, guiding thee
 into the Heaven afar!—
Alone I stray by the mountain walls that support the enamelled
 mirror-sky,
Enfolding my free-born soul in the vice-purifying odours of the forest
 from an unknown corner of Paradise.
Art thirsty?—here rolls the snow-robed water for thy fulfillment;
Does dullness veil thee?—here a stone chamber invites thee into the
 world of dreams through an unseen door.
O return, brother mortal, from Samsara unto the great Valley!
Yea, the mighty Temple of the World, everlasting with the heaven and
 earth, welcomes thee!
Behold! Yosemite, sermoning Truth and Liberty, battles in spirit with
 the Pacific Ocean afar!
O unfading wonder, eternal glory! I pray a redemption from the
 majesty that chains me—

(Lo, Hell offers a great edifice unto Heaven!) O, I bid my envy and
   praise rest against thee;

I am content in the sounding Silence, in the powerless Time that
   holds the Valley in the age of gold;

I proffer my stainful body and leprous soul with blackest shame unto
   thee;

I am united with the Universe, and the Universe with me.

O hail, brother mortal! the true joy is revealed unto thee—

Be thou a wave ebbing and flowing with the air of Heaven!

Behold! The genii of the forest chant Peace unto the Lord from an
   unknown shrine in the Valley temple.

O mighty chapel of God! Thou knowest not an iron chariot stained
   with hostile blood;—

Aye, idle spears and foolish shields dare not ruin thee, proclaiming
   War in Eternity!

Song of Night in Yosemite Valley

Hark! The prophecy-inciting windquake of the unfathomable concave
 of darkest Hell!
O, the God-scorning demon's shout against the truth-locked gate of
 mighty Heaven!
Heaven and Hell joining their palace and dungeon, remould the sinful
 universe to an ethereal paradise—
O, the sphere is shaken by the Master-Mechanic working from the
 surface of the world to its center!
Alas, the sun has fled in saddest woe!—O mortal, breathe thy silent
 prayer unto mighty Yosemite for mirth!
Behold, the light of day leaves the white mansion to the care of
 dolorous night!—
The genii of the Valley fly from the roar of a thousand lions to the
 sacred peace above—
Lo, an unknown jeweller decks the black, velvety heaven with
 treasure-stars—
Yea, the Mother-Goddess, mantling the earth with the night, forbids
 Yosemite disturb her baby-angel's dream in the heaven!
Hark! the night disconcord of the eternal falling of waters sounding
 discontent throughout the earth—
O, a chariot is rushing down to an unknown hollow in wild triumph!
Behold, a dragon reveals divinity in the ghostly-odorous sky of night—
Nay, the mighty sword of the Judgment Day blazes down the Heaven
 to the gate of Hell!

FROM "FROM THE EASTERN SEA" (1903)

APPARITION

'Twas morn;
 I felt the whiteness of her brow
 Over my face; I raised my eyes and saw
 The breezes passing on dewy feet.

'Twas noon;
 Her slightly trembling lips of passion
 I saw, I felt, but where she smiled
 Were only yellow flakes of sunlight.

'Twas eve;
 The velvet shadows of her hair enforded me;
 I eagerly stretched my hand to grasp her,
 But touched the darkness of eve.

'Twas night;
 I heard her eloquent violet eyes
 Whispering love, but from the heaven
 Gazed down the stars in gathering tears.

O Cho San

Dream was in the soul of the garden brook,
Spring in its song: O Cho San
Leaned her down to face her image
In the brook; both smiled in greeting.
In sudden thought she looked behind;
The sadness of a midnight star
Abode in her unmoving eyes;
The mists of silence filled the gate of her lips.
The moments slipped by: the sunlight fell
Over her face, as a golden message;
The kiss of beauty graced her hair;
The soft odour of womanhood beautifully rose;
The butterflies surrounding her forgot to part:
She was in indolence. Slowly she
Began a dreamy smile, silently facing
Toward a calm sea of fancy: her smile
Was that of an April-night cherry-blossom
To the wind. Softly she looked round and whispered:
"At the return of my lord I will thus smile.
My sweet lover, when Anata shall return!"
And smiling bravely with a sweet intent, she said:
"Look what a beautiful smiling O Cho San!"
Then much she blushed, and started up, and, with a sigh,
Began a languid, graceful walk along the path:
Her walk was that of an afternoon breeze
With the fragrance of cherry-blossoms.
The petals of the flower, like butterflies,
Abruptly fell, some on her shoulders
And her hair; the brook gossiped of Spring.
She walked amid the solemn loveliness of eve:
And solitude and dreams were with her soul;
Dim poems rose around her like odours
Unto the moon. She was beautiful as one
Who smiling, enters in the gate of Sorrow:
The earth upturned her melancholy face

Toward the heavens the evening bell
Tolled as the last song of a sea.
"Beloved! Beloved!" she cried;
Her streaming eyes beheld a silent star.

Address to a Soyokaze*

O Soyokaze,
From the golden bower of the morning sun,
In gracefully loose gown,
Your eyes strewing the wealth of aerial beauty
That is half shadow, half odour,
Up with me, Soyokaze!
I've left behind the mortal love,
And all the books dear next to woman.
Up, up, and seek with me
A thousand stars
Lost beyond the skies!
Sail afar with me,
O Soyokaze, on light-gleaming step;
Sail into the garden strange yet my own!
I'll build there my home in the moonbeams,
I'll gather the poems from the flowers,
And from the hearts of birds.
Sail, sail, my Soyokaze!
When I am tired,
We'll rest, my head on your shoulder,
And I'll listen to your tales
That you heard under the roses
Passing through the woodland.
When the tree throws its shadow on the ground
(The shadow is its written song),
And I see not its real meaning,
You will instantly rise,
And play the harp of the leaves,
And make me fully understland.
O beloved Soyokaze,
My dear comrade,
Be with my soul eternally
Since I am sundered from the world,
And am alone!

---

* "Soyokaze" is "zephyr" in Japanese.

YONE NOGUCHI

Under the Moon

The autumn night had a sad impressive beauty.
I turned my face as a flower,
In indolence: the sweet mystery of indolence
Whispered me an alien legend I, with lips apart,
With the large mindless eyes, stood
As one fresh from a fairy dream:
The ecstacy of the dream was not yet dry
On my face. The strangest stillness,
As exquisite as if all the winds
Were dead, surrounded me; I idly thought,
What a poem, and what love were hidden behind
The moon, and how great to be beyond mortal breath,
Far from the human domain. My moon-fancy,
Aimless as a breeze of summer eve,
Drowsy as a rose of Spring morning, has passed:
My fancy was a fragrance as from an unknown isle
Where Beauty smiled her favourite smile.
How glad I was, being wounded by
The beautiful rush of yellow rays!
The sad sobbing charm of the moon
Was that of the face of an ancient fairy.
The moon gracefully kept her perfect silence
Until a greater muse shall restore the world
From demon's sword and unworthy death.
I was in the lullaby of the moon,
As a tree snugly wrapped in the mist:
I lost all my earthly thoughts.
The moon was voiceless as a nun
With eyes shining in beauteous grief:
The mystic silence of the moon
Gradually revived in me the Immortality,
The sorrow that gently stirred
Was melancholy-sweet: sorrow is higher
Far than joy, the sweetest sorrow is supreme
Amid all the passions. I had
No sorrow of mortal heart: my sorrow

Was one given before the human sorrows
Were given me. Mortal speech died
From me: my speech was one spoken before
God bestowed on me human speech.
There is nothing like the moon-night
When I, parted from the voice of the city,
Drink deep of Infinity with peace
From another, a stranger sphere. There is nothing
Like the moon-night when the rich noble stars
And maiden roses interchange their long looks of love.
There is nothing like the moon-night
When I raise my face from the land of loss
Unto the golden air, and calmly learn
How perfect it is to grow still as a star.
There is nothing like the moon-night
When I walk upon the freshest dews,
And amid the warmest breezes,
With all the thought of God
And all the bliss of man, as Adam
Not yet driven from Eden, and to whom
Eve was not yet born. What a bird
Dreams in the moonlight is my dream:
What a rose sings is my song.

O HANA SAN

It was many and many a year ago,
In a garden of the cherry-blossom
Of a far-off isle you may know
By the fairy name of Nippon,
That a maiden who was dressing her hair
Against the mirror of a shining spring,
Casting over me her sudden heavenly glance,
Entreated me to break a beautiful branch
Of the cherry-tree: I cannot forget.
I was a boy on the way home
From my school; I threw aside
All my books and slate, and I climbed
Up the tree, and looked down
Over her little anxious butterfly face:
Oh, how the wind blew fanning me
With a love that was more than earthly love,
In a garden of the cherry-blossom
Of a far-off isle you may know
By the fairy name of Nippon!
I broke a branch, slowly dropped it
To her up-raised hands that God shaped
With best art and pain; she smiled
Toward me an angel smile; she,
Speaking no word, ran away as a breeze,
Leaving behind the silver evening moon,
And hid from me in the shadow of a pine-tree
In a garden of the cherry-blossom
Of a far-off isle you may know
By the fairy name of Nippon.
I stole toward her on tiptoe.
As a silent moonbeam to a sleeping flower,
And frightened her with a shout of "Mitsuketa wa,"*
And I ran away from her, smiling and blushing,
In a garden of the cherry-blossom

---

* "I found thee out" in English.

Of a far-off isle you may know
By the fairy name of Nippon.
And I hid me beneath the gate of a temple,
That was a pathway to the heavens.
She stepped softly as the night,
Found me and looked upon me with a smile like a star.
Tapped my head with the branch,
Speaking fondly, "My sweetest one!"
I had no answer but a glad laugh
That was taught by the happy wind
In a garden of the cherry-blossom
Of a far-off isle you may know
By the fairy name of Nippon.
And that maiden who was known
By the pretty name of O Hana San,
Ran away gracefully as a Spring cloud
Into the heavens, blushing and smiling,
Then I followed O Hana's steps,
Into the heavens, into the realm of Love.

The Myoto*

The woman whispered in the voice that roses have lost:
"My love!"
The man said, "Yes, dear!"
In the voice that seas cannot utter.

The woman whispered in the voice of velvet-footed moon-beams:
"My love!"
The man said, "Yes, dear!"
In the voice that mountains keep in bosom.

The woman whispered in the voice of eve calling the stars to appear:
"My love!"
The man said, "Yes, dear!"
In the voice of dawn for Spring and Life.

The woman whispered in the voice of a young summer rivulet:
"My love!"
The man said, "Yes, dear!"
In the voice of forests unto the sky.

---

* "Myoto" is Japanese for "couple" in English.

The Goddess: God

The goddess spins the wool of the rivulet to its length:
O silver song of the female spinner!
O golden silence of the male spinner!
God spinning with the wheel of Time,
White of day and darkness of the night to eternity.

By the Sea

The moon came sadly out of a hill;
I from the city silently stole:
Many an hour had passed since I shook
The sorrow-thoughts to the winds.
The moon's beautiful cold steps were my steps,
In silvery peace, apart from paths of men:
The dewy mysterious beams, as love-whispers,
Stole in my hair which zephyr stirred
As cloud; I was as in the mazy sweet,
I knew not why. I smiled unto the moon;
The moon understood me: the silence was profound.
On the sea-face unearthly dreams
And greenly melancholic autumn voicelessly stepped:
The moon threw a large soft smile over the sea.
The sea was verily proud to sing:
The sea's passions wooing the shore,
Taught me the secret how to win woman;
But the love of woman was left far behind.
I slowly thought how beautiful to sink
Into the moon-sea and to rise
With worshipping face unto the moon:
A sea-bird suddenly sprung from the wave,
Scattering sea-pearls with lavish wing.
I sat me down on the shore,
With tragic eyes upon the stars,
With my ears unto the sea:
The silence of the stars was as great
As the voice of the sea; it is so
Since the First day, that the stars
Keep the silence and the sea the voice.
I walked with the moon, by the sea,
Till the dawn: what I thought was that
The moon thought, I knew not what.

Homekotoba*

I

I hear, O lovely lady, in thy voice,
The music of a hidden flower valley,
Anear yet distant; from thy face
The beauty of Spring flashes:
I linger around thee, faithful and ecstatic.
The murmur of a rose,
Or of a white star that peeps
Out of another world of poetry,
Is the murmur of thy gracious eyes:
Thine eyes are veiled by the misty breezes.
Thy lips of infinity are beautifully wet
With human kisses and with the breath of life;
On thy cheeks bloom the flowers of moonbeams;
Thy bosom holds the mystery of the sky;
The laughter of the air is thy laughter.
The freshness of a sea at morn
Is like unto thy fragrant thought of woman;
A wood with leaves glistening with dewdrops
And a singing bird are symbols of thy fancy;
A flower of morning prayer is thy upturned look
Into the sunlight that, like organ melody,
Rolls up the vault of heaven from the east;
On thy hair flutters the gossip of heaven.
A vision of heavenly beauty in a haze
Is thy lithe form reclining upon the grasses;
A lily appearing from the gossamer
Is thy face looking out from the bewilderment;
Thy soul is a divine complexity
In which I lose my way as in a dream.
Thy smile was born in light of summer blessedness;
The dark-browed wind in Spring rain is thy melancholy:

---

* "Homekotoba" means "praising words."

YONE NOGUCHI

Thy breath is the whisper along a violet road;
Thy shadow on my breast is thy heart's history.

II

I read, O lovely lady, in thy face
All the religions of beauty
(They are nothing else but Love);
Thy silence musical and commanding
Is that of a harp set in the windless air.
Whenever I see thee my new page of life begins,
With the moon of another light,
With the fresh stir of a new field of wealth;
If I was not born for anything else,
I was born with one aim to adore thee:
One aim is enough for any life.
Thy head is thrust up into the breath of gods,
Yet thy feet on the dandelion ground;
Each pool of the sky woos thy beauty,
Every shadow of earth-tree gossips of thee;
The fancy road of thy song I pursue,
I loiter in the blessed vale of thy heart.
O how proud I feel to see thy face
Hasting to meet my face, as a flower
Hurries to the silken shower of sunshine!
I dare to say that thou art fed
With my praising words lavished over thee:
I dream in the odour of thy womanhood.
Since thou belongst me, my life begins
To be very important; I have to walk
Safely on the clear road of emerald light,
Safely along the flower-rimmed path of poesy.
With thy hand upon thy bosom,
I will feel all the mystery of thy love;
With my hand upon my brow,
I ask thee what a confidence thou feelst in me;
Casting two shadows on the stream of Life,
We will whistle of the sweet world to the moon.

III

Thy divinely large eyes, O lovely lady,
Gaze beyond our world into a hid kingdom
Of coral-hued beauty and sapphire thought;
The fragrance from thy lips which are a rose
Speaks more than thy golden speech:
The gossamers tarry around thy rose-lips.
Thou seemst unto me a vaporous beauty
Which I saw upon the Spring seas,
Laying me down on the silvery sand of the shore,
With my soul in the song of the seas;
I fear that thou mayest vanish any moment:
What a fear and joy I feel
In my sacred marriage with thee!
The moon marred by clouds is beautiful:
Joy mingled with fear has a deeper thrill.
How often before my lips opened,
Wishing thy impressive kisses;
How often before my hands stretched,
Wishing to feel thy deep bosom:
I ever dreamed of thee amid the breezes,
Under the shadows of flowers and stars:
If my present union with thee be a dream,
The dream has to be eternal.
Everything has a silent hour at whiles:
'Tis sweet to bathe in the silence by thy side;
'Tis sweeter to raise the head from the sea-silence,
And to stare on thy high-born face,
Like a sea-ear gatherer on the sea-waves
With eyes turned toward the abandoned shore.
Then in the stillness of eve (yet stirring
Enough to make one sweetly sad), I
Bind my body with thine own, and send
My soul along the road of the Divine Unseen.

IV

The soul of flower, O lovely lady,
Is the soul of poem; the soul of poem
Is thy soul: thou art like a faithful-eyed caravan
Across the waste, bringing heavenly jewels.
The winds come from east and west,
But thy wind of heart only comes from
The singing woodland of Love.
The air around thy bosom grows roseate
By the fire within; from the ground
Under thy feet has blossomed a daffodil:
Thy presence is the presence of Sun.
My old memory and new dream jauntily come
Riding on thy eye-flash of pearl:
Thou art the soul of all the dawns.
In thy soul I see a brook
Whose song of silvery happiness I love most,
Since I tired of iron-buskined song;
Thy soul with a far-away voice
Like that of an eve of a thousand stars,
Calls me to a task of high yearning;
I see my face in the mirror of thy heart,
And triumphantly smile, thinking that
I am thy husband and slave.
Under the tree-shade I lay me down,
And smell thy balsam breath stealing
Around me like a sweet ancient tale;
Upturning my face I draw
Thy lovely shape in the purple sky:
Since I love thee, my life grows plain,
My dream being only to be faithful to thee,
My toil being only to entertain thee.
The life of simplicity is the life of beauty:
With the beauty and with thee I remain forever.

Upon the Heights

And victor of life and silence,
I stood upon the Heights; triumphant,
With upturned eyes, I stood,
And smiled unto the sun, and sang
A beautifully sad farewell unto the dying day,
And my thoughts and the eve gathered
Their serpentine mysteries around me,
My thoughts like alien breezes,
The eve like a fragrant legend.
My feeling was that I stood as one
Serenely poised for flight, as a muse
Of golden melody and lofty grace.
Yea, I stood as one scorning the swords
And wanton menace of the cities.
The sun had heavily sunk into the seas beyond,
And left me a tempting sweet and twilight.
The eve with trailing shadows westward
Swept on, and the lengthened shadows of trees
Disappeared: how silently the songs of silence
Steal into my soul! And still I stood
Among the crickets, in the beateous profundity
Sung by stars; and I saw me
Softly melted into the eve. The moon
Slowly rose: my shadow on the ground
Dreamily began a dreamy roam,
And I upward smiled silent welcome.

The Poet

Out of the deep and the dark,
A sparkling mystery, a shape,
Something perfect,
Comes like the stir of the day:
One whose breath is an odour,
Whose eyes show the road to stars,
The breeze in his face,
The glory of Heaven on his back.
He steps like a vision hung in air,
Diffusing the passion of Eternity;
His abode is the sunlight of morn,
The music of eve his speech:
In his sight,
One shall turn from the dust of the grave,
And move upward to the woodland.

The Face in the Mirror

"Why do you cry so, dear little girl?
 Come, dry your tears," I said,
"Like a dew-bathed butterfly in the sun rays,
 And then tell me of yourself."
 The girl said:
"My kind Danna San, 'twas this morn
 When the breath of Spring blew along the mountain path,
 That I went up alone to gather wild-flowers,
 And there naughty neighbour's children shouted at me:
"Look at that dirty motherless girl!"
 Then I retorted that I had my mother in the mirror,
 And I ran home and I saw the mirror,—
 Alas! my mother's face was crying,
 Because I cried.
 Then I felt still more sad,
 And cried still more,
 And now still I cry."
 I said to the girl:
"Sweet child, the face in the mirror
 Is not your mother's, but your own."
 The girl flinging a quick opposing look,
 Impatiently said:
"So many many years older than I you are,
 So much more wiser than I you are,
 But, my great lord, you know nothing of my mirror.
 The face in the mirror is mother's,
 So mother said:
 My dear mother never told a lie.
 The mirror was left me
 When she died, and she said:
 'Whenever you want to see me,
 You'll find me in the mirror,
 I a thousand times have looked in it,
 And hidden there my truest face.'
 Since then, every eve at dusk,
 When the church bell sounds to me like mother's call,

I hurry to my mirror,
And I see my mother looking at me."
Then I said:
"Listen, dear little maiden,
I will adorn your hair with the flowers,
I will give you money for a new Spring dress,
And you shall smile, that's a good girl!
Aren't you happy?
Now look at your mirror, gentle child."
The girl looked in the mirror, and joyfully exclaimed:
"Mother is happy,
Because I am happy.
I'll not cry any more,
You'll cry no more, my dear mother."
Then we lay down in the sunlight,
With her pretty head on my knee.
I told many a tale of fairy queens far and near.
My voice was music to her ears,
Her head languidly drooped,
Her innocent sleeping face in the mirror by her side:
I saw the breezes playing with the tassels of her hair.

How near to Fairyland

The spring warmth steals into me, drying up all the tears of my soul,
And gives me a flight into the vastness,—into a floorless, unroofed
reverie-hall.

Lo, such greenness, such velvety greenness, such a heaven without
heaven above!
Lo, again, such grayness, such velvety grayness, such an earth without
earth below!
My soul sails through the waveless mirror-seas.

Oh, how near to Fairyland!
Blow, blow, gust of wind!
Sweep away my soul-boat against that very shore!

LINES

I love the saintly chant of the winds touching their odorous fingers to
    the harp of the angel Spring;
I love the undiscording sound of thousands of birds, whose concord of
    song echoes on the rivulet afar;
I muse on the solemn mountain which waits in sound content for the
    time when the Lord calls forth;
I roam with the wings of high-raised fantasy in the pure universe;
Oh, I chant of the garden of Adam and Eve!

Spring

Spring,
Winged Spring,
A laughing butterfly,
Flashes away,
Rosy-cheeked Spring,
Angel of a moment.
The little shadow of my lover perfumed,
Maiden Spring,
Now fades,
The shadew,
The golden shadow,
With all the charm.
Spring,
Naughty sweet Spring,
A proud coquette,
Born to laugh but not to live,
Spring,
Flying Spring,
A beautiful runaway,
Leaves me in tears,
But my soul follows after,
Till I catch her.
Next March.
Spring,
Spring!

FROM "THE SUMMER CLOUDS" (1906)

Prose Poems

"The Summer clouds rise in shape of fantastic peaks."

I

WAVE, WAVE, BLACK HAIR OF my Beauty, wave, and wave, and show me where the love deepens, and the forest silence thickens; show me where Peace is buried with heavy wings, and where hours never grow gray!

Wave, wave, black hair of my Beauty, wave, and wave, and show me where the shadows are gold, and the airs are honey, show me the heart—joy of Life and world; wave and wave, black hair of my Beauty!

II

TOUCH ME WITH THY SOFT hands, O Yuki San! They are soft as moonbeams on the singing sands, O Yuki San! They are soft as kisses of the eve, thy soft hands; they are soft as rivulets over the Spring lands, O Yuki San!

Oh, touch me again with thy soft hands, O Yuki San! I feel the passion and Truth of forgotten ages in their touches, O Yuki San! I feel the songs and incense in their touches, O Yuki San!

Here by the sea I sit from dawn till the dusk, O Yuki San! I dream of thy soft hands, soft as soft foams on the laughing shore, O Yuki San! The sun is gone and the soft moon is rising, but never thy soft hands again, O Yuki San!

III

THE RAIN STOPPED SUDDENLY, WHEN the moon made her way in the sky. O Moon! thou art not the ball of fire and poetry, but thou art the mirror of my Lady Beauty who imparts her own Beauty and Truth, day and night!

Here upon the garden of roses (roses are my Lady Beauty's favourite flowers) I stand. My soul rises from the odours and earth, and comes close to the moon. O Moon! my Lady Beauty's mirror, make my soul and Love nobler by Beauty and Truth which my Lady Beauty imparts.

I think only of my Lady Beauty whose work of life was to turn my soul and Love to gold. Oh, where is she, this very moment?

IV

OUT OF THE GRAY FOREST (Forest? It is the forest. But I doubt whether it was not a shadow) I hear the gray voice of a bird. Oh, lonely bird, art thou still sad? Art thou still keeping comradeship with Death and Darkness? So am I—a poet quietly leaning on the wall of sadness. I burn incense and pray once in a while. How afraid I am to stir up the air of silence! Spring is coming so slow. My soul is kissing the Heart of Voicelessness.

I hear the gray voice of the bird sinking and sinking far down like a dead leaf. Where does it go? It is like my soul which started somewhere without purpose, and is sailing without end. Oh, where does my soul aim to go?

And again I hear another gray voice of another bird out of the gray forest.

Dear lonely Voice, tell me where thou want'st to go! Art thou going into the silver temple of the immortal moonlight? Art thou going into the dusky bosom of the Mother-Rest? Pray, take my soul with thee, O comrade!

V

THE HAPPY LITTLE SONGS GO to-day under the arms of a wind: my heart will go with them, wherever they go. As the little voices of the leaves they go, laughing and singing. Now they are suddenly still, when the white dews fall under the stars. Is it not the time for them to hurry to their beds in the House of Peace by the mountain flowers? My heart will be happy and go with them wherever they go.

VI

I HEAR YOU CALL, PINE-TREE, I hear you upon the hill; by the silent pond where the lotos flowers bloom, I hear you call, Pine-tree!

What is it you call, Pine-tree, when the rains fall, when the winds blow, and when the stars appear, what is it you call, Pine-tree?

I hear you call, Pine-tree, but I am blind, and do not know how to reach you, Pine-tree. Who will take me to you, Pine-tree?

VII

OUT OF THE CRADLE OF great Silence, from under the grave (do you feel Silence's touch?) the poet, the singer of Seen and Unseen, still sings his voiceless song—the song of the land of shadow and agelessness, the song of the land of peace and memory, the song of the land of Silence and mist! I hear, O poet, thy new melody of voicelessness, thy sweet song of eternal Spring eve, thy song like that of the moon over the land of sleep, thy song of Heaven and love! O poet, thy song fills my heart with sweet unrest and with dreams like passing clouds! O poet, thy song comes from under the grave—out of the cradle of Silence, like the flowing tide!

VIII

THE SPRING FIELD, CALM, ODOROUS, like the breast of Heaven, waving in red and green, like a flowing sea in tune of breeze. A thousand birds, like ships, singing of Spring hope, searching after a joyous life. (O bird-ships on the newest sea!)

"What news, speak, dear ships from another land?"

"Only a love-message, my lord!"

IX

I AND NATURE ARE ONE in sweet weariness: my soul slowly fades into Sleep. Is this earth? Or Heaven? The summer odour sweetens Nature to dream: the trees and birds murmur with a breeze.

"I am blind, deaf, and also dumb; I am a traveller toward God, alas! without a guide," I say.

Oh, deathlessness! Oh, happiness! I and Summer spirits play upon a vast sea of fancy.

FROM "THE PILGRIMAGE" (1909)

"THE NEW ART"

She is an art (let me call her so)
Hung as a web in the air of perfume,
Soft yet vivid, she sways in music:
(But what sadness in her saturation of life!)
Her music lives in the intensity of a moment, and then dies;
To her suggestion is life.
She left behind the quest of beauty and dream;
Is her own self not the song of dream and beauty itself?
(I know she is tired of ideal and problem and talk.)
She is the moth-light playing on reality's dusk,
Soon to die as a savage prey of the moment;
She is a creation of surprise (let me say so),
Dancing gold on the wire of impulse.
What an elf of light and shadow!
What a flash of tragedy and beauty!

By the Engakuji Temple: Moon Night

Through the breath of perfume,
(O music of musics!)
Down creeps the moon
To fill my cup of song
With memory's wine.

Across the song of night and moon,
(O perfume of perfumes!)
My soul, as a wind
Whose heart's too full to sing,
Only roams astray . . ,

Down the tide of the sweet night
(O the ecstasy's gentle rise!)
The birds, flowers and trees
Are glad at once to fall
Into Oblivion's ruin white.

To a Nightingale

Creator of the only one song!
Triumph, rapture and art thou tellest
But with thy self-same word, what mystery!
I have a few more songs and dreams than thou,
(Alas, my words not serving at my command!)
I tremble, hesitate before I sing:
What carelessness in thy rush with song,
Splendour is thine to sing into air, be forgotten!
Thou singest out, thou pushest thy song's way,
Without regard to the others waiting their turns,
(Pity the other birds and poets!)
What a sweet bit of thy barbarism!
I know not technically what thy song means:
I take thee not only for a bird but the poet.
Thou art a revolter against prosody:
What a discoverer of the newest language!
A man's life and art are disturbed by thy song,
(What exhaustion in thy voice,
What a feast and sensation of thy life!)
When thou changest him to become thy kin,—
A thing of simplicity and force;
Thy song stops, thou fliest away.
Oh, can thy work be done so swift?
Didst thou see thy song's future in him?
Thou art suggestion: what a fragment of art!

I am Like a Leaf

The silence is broken: into the nature
    My soul sails out,
Carrying the song of life on his brow,
    To meet the flowers and birds.

When my heart returns in the solitude,
    She is very sad,
Looking back on the dead passions
    Lying on Love's ruin.

I am like a leaf
    Hanging over hope and despair,
Which trembles and joins
    The world's imagination and ghost.

To the Sunflower

Thou burstest from mood:
How sad we have to cling to experience!
Marvel of thy every atom burning of life,
How fully thou livest!
Didst thou ever think to turn to cold and shadow?
Passionate liver of sunlight,
Symbol of youth and pride;
Thou art a lyric of thy soaring colour;
Thy voicelessness of song is action.
What absorption of thy life's meaning,
Wonder of thy consciousness,—
Mighty sense of thy existence!

Shadow

My song is sung, but a moment. . .
The song of voice is merely the body, (the body dies,)
And the real part of the song, its soul, remains after it is sung:
Yea, it remains in the vibration of thy waves of heart-sea
Echoing still my song, (O shadow my song threw!)
In thy heart's thrill I see my far truer and whiter soul,
And through my soul thou soarest out of thy dust and griefs.

. . . Spring passed,
(Spring in roses and birds is merely the body,)
And I see the greater Spring (O soul-shadow she left!)
In the Summer forest, luminous in green and dream:
Oh to be that Spring over the word's Summer valley,
O shadow I may cast in the after-age, O my shadow of soul!

The Fantastic Snow-flakes

Bah! What fantastic snow-flakes, eh,
Dancing merrily, ha! ha! ha!
Lo, their tiny feet raising so!

Death is sweet, to be sure,
Laughing they go to death,
What delicious teeth, ha! ha! ha!

Suppose we die together, eh,
With the snow dying upon a pond?
What a fantastic end, ha! ha! ha!

What a fantastic end to die
In the dying music of ancient love!
Behold the snow and music die!

What a coward, ha! ha! ha!
Are you afraid to die, eh?
Still you love a little caprice of world?

What fantastic snow-flakes, ha! ha! ha!
To leave no sorrow and to die!
Such a coward, you my beloved!

GHOST OF ABYSS

My dreams rise when the rain falls: the sudden songs
Flow about my ears as the clouds in June;
And the footsteps, lighter than the heart of wind,
Beat, now high, then low, before my dream-flaming eyes.

"Who am I?" said I. "Ghost of abyss," a Voice replied,
"Piling an empty stone of song on darkness of night,
 Dancing wild as a fire, only to vanish away."

Autumn Song

The gold vision of a bird-wind sways on the silver foam of song,
The oldest song rises again on the Autumn heart of dream.

The ghost castle of glory is built by the sad magic of Time,
With the last laughter of sorrow, and with the red tempest of leaves.

My little soul born out of the dews of singing dawn,
Bids farewell to the large seas of Life and speech.

Fantasia

Bits of straw and clay and woman's hair,—
So shall be builded my house:
Oh to lose the world and gain a song!
Let the clouds flit through the window at the left;
The dancer shapeless in pain and pride,
From the right dance in as a tide:
A spirit of pagan days, sick in joy,
That rose at the sound of their stamping feet,
I'll sing a song that makes the seas the hills.
(Morality begins, I am afraid, where I stop my song.)
Rags to roll me in, pieces of dream,
So with my heart of nocturnal fear;
I have chose of the sky red in memory and art.
Let the stars fall in the garden rose:
The leaves and my souls in a thousand guises
Hurry to the ground to build a grave.

The Temple Bell

Trembling in its thousand ages,
Dark as its faith,
It wails, hunting me,
(It's a long time since I lost my faith,)
Up through the silence with a scorn,
Heavy but not unkind,
Out of the dusk of the temple and night
Into my heart of dusk,
Hushed after my song of cities played,
Weary and grey in thought.
My heart replies to the wail of the bell,
Slow-bosomed in sadness and faith,
With my memory rising from dusts,
Namu amida butsu! Namu amida butsu!

To the Cicada

What a sudden pain of ancient soul,—
A tear that is a voice, a voice that is a tear!
What unforgotten tragedy thou tellest in thy break of heart!
Min min, min, min, minminminminmin. . . !

Grey singer of the forest with heart of fire,
Dost thou cry for the world, or for my love and life?
Is thy monotony of voice the tragedy of my song?
Min, min, min, min, minminminminmin. . . !

The soul that reads the sorrow of life knows thy heart:
Cry till the world and life gain the triumph of death!
Let us earn Death through the tragedy of Faith!
O singer of sad Faith and only one song,—
Cry out thy old dream of life and tears!
Min, min, min, min, minminminminmin. . . !

The Lady of Utamaro's Art

Too common to say she is the beauty of line,
However, the line old, spiritualised into odour,
(The odour soared into an everlasting ghost from life and death,)
As a gossamer, the handiwork of dream,
'Tis left free as it flaps:
The lady of Utamaro's Art is the beauty of zephyr flow.
I say again, the line with the breath of love,
Enwrapping my heart to be a happy prey:
Sensuous? To some so she may appear,
But her sensuousness divinised into the word of love.
To-day I am with her in silence of twilight eve,
And am afraid she may vanish into the mist.

The Buddha Priest in Meditation

He is a style of monotony,
His religion is aloofness,
Is there any simplicity more beautiful?
What a grand leisure in his walk
On the road of mystery:
Is there any picture more real,
More permanent than he?
He surrenders against faith:
He walks on mystery's road,—that is enough,
He never quests why.
He feels a touch beyond word,
He reads the silence's sigh,
And prays before his own soul and destiny:
He is a pseudonym of the universal consciousness,
A person lonesome from concentration.
He is possessed of Nature's instinct,
And burns white as a flame;
His morality and accident of life
No longer exist,
But only the silence and soul of prayer.

In the Inland Sea

Here the waters of wine with far-off desires,
Here the April breezes with purple flashes familiar and yet forgotten,
Oh, here the twilight of the Inland Sea!
Here I hear a song without a word,
(Is it the song of my flying soul?)
That's the song of my dream I dreamed a thousand years ago,
Oh, my dream of the fairy world, oh, the beauty of the Inland Sea!
I sail and sail to-day in this fairy sea,
(O my heart, hear the sailors' song of life!)
I sail leaving the welcoming isles far behind,
(Hear the isles bidding adieu, O my heart!)
I sail toward the chanting sky.
O birds with white souls, steer my soul with white love,
Here the sea of my dream, Oh, the beauty of the Inland Sea!

Kyoto

Mist-born Kyoto, the city of scent and prayer,
Like a dream half-fading, she lingers on:
The oldest song of a forgotten pagoda bell
Is the Kamo River's twilight song.

The girls, half whisper and half love,
As old as a straying moonbeam,
Flutter on the streets gods built,
Lightly carrying Spring and passion.

"Stop a while with me," I said.
They turned their powdered necks. How delicious!
"No, thank you, some other time," they replied.
Oh, such a smile like the breath of a rose!

My Little Bird

My little bird,
My bird born in my Mother's tears,
She flies,
Stretching her wings so,
And from under her wings she drops my Mother's message:
"Come home, Beloved!"

Running out from my Mother's bosom,
My little river,
She suddenly stopped her song,
And looking up to the sun,
She in her ripples flashed my Mother's message:
"Beloved, come home!"

My roses,
My little roses grow in my Mother's breath,
They are sad to-day,
Casting their faces down;
On their petals I read my Mother's message:
"Come home, Beloved!"

Her Weapons are a Smile and
a Little Fan

Her weapons are a smile and a little fan.
Sayonara, sayonara . . .
Her bent neck like that of a stork
Seeking a jewel of heart in the ground!
Her wisdom is folded sweet in her bosom.
Sayonara, sayonara . . .
Her flapping robe like a cloud
That follows a lyric of butterfly!
Her song is on her tips of naked feet.
Sayonara, sayonara. . .
Beat of her wooden clogs
Playing the unseen strings of love!

My Heart

Oh Lord, is it the reflection of my heart of fire?
Is it, my Lord, the sunset flashes of the Western sky?
Oh Lord, is it the echo of my heart of unrest?
Is it, my Lord, the cry of a sea breaking on the sand?
Oh Lord, is it the voice of my sorrowful heart?
Is it, my Lord, the wail of a wind seeking the road in the dark?
Oh Lord, is it the dripping tears of my heart?
Is it, my Lord, the rain carrying tragedy from the Heavens?

The Lotus Worshippers

From dale and hill the worshippers steal
In whitest robes: yea, with whitest souls.
They sit around the holy pond, the lotus home,
Their finger-tips folded like the hushing lotus-buds
Thrust through the water and twilight, nun-like,
And they pray (the silent prayer that is higher than the prayer of
    speech).
The stars and night suddenly cease their song,
The air and birds begin to stir.
(O Resurrection, Resurrection of World and Life!)
Lo, Sun ascending! The lotus buds flash with hearts parted,
With one chant "Namu, Amida!"
The stars disappear, nay, they fall in their hearts.
The worshippers turn their silent steps toward their homes,
Learning that the stars will fall in their truthful souls,
And the road of sunlight is the road of prayer,
And for Paradise.
Their faces shining under the sun's blessing gold,
They chant the divine name along the woodland.

Lines

The sun I worship,
Not for the light, but for the shadows of the trees he draws:
O shadows welcome like an angel's bower,
Where I build Summer-day dreams!
Not for her love, but for the love's memory,
The woman I adore;
Love may die, but not the memory eternally green—
The well where I drink Spring ecstasy.
To a bird's song I listen,
Not for the voice, but for the silence following after the song:
O Silence fresh from the bosom of voice!—
Melody from the Death-Land whither my face does ever turn!

The Eastern Sea

I say my farewell to the Western cities;
I will return to the Eastern Sea,—
To my isle kissed first ever by the sun,—
I will now go to my sweetest home,
And lay there my griefs on a mountain's breast,
And give all my songs to the birds, and sleep long
A wind may stir the forest, I may awake,
I will whistle my joy of life up to a cloud:
The life of the cloud will be my life there.
How tall my lover now will be!
She was two inches shorter than I long ago.
When mid the wistarias the moon-lantern is lit,
She and I will steal to measure our heights
By their drooping flowers—drooping calm like peace.
Should she win, I will pay her my kisses seven:
I will take her seven kisses if I win:
So all the same the kisses shall be mine.
Then we will walk by the idols—the saint's and the poet's,
And assure them that Life is but Love;
With Love and chrysanthemum I will remain forever.

To a Sparrow

Sudden ghost
That danced out again from the shadow and rest,
Hunter of the memory and colour of thy last life,
Dost thou find the same humanity, the same dream?
Consecrator of every moment,
Holder of the genius for living,
Thy one moment might be our ten years:
Does it tempt, console and frighten thee?
Ghost of nerve,
If thy voice be curse,
It is with all thy soul.
If it be repentance,
It is with all thy body.
Oh, would that I could relish the same sensation as thou!

Right and Left

The mountain green at my right:
The sunlight yellow at my left:
The laughing winds pass between.

The river white at my left:
The flowers red at my right:
The laughing girls go between.

The clouds sail away at my right:
The birds flap down at my left:
The laughing moon appears between.

I turned left to the dale of poem;
I turned right to the forest of Love:
But I hurry Home by the road between.

IN JAPAN BEYOND

Do you not hear the sighing of a willow in Japan,
(In Japan beyond, in Japan beyond)
In the voice of a wind searching for the sun lost,
For the old faces with memory in eyes?

Do you not hear the sighing of a bamboo in Japan,
(In Japan beyond, in Japan beyond)
In the voice of a sea urging with the night,
For the old dreams of a twilight tale?

Do you not hear the sighing of a pine in Japan,
(In Japan beyond, in Japan beyond)
In the voice of a river in quest of the Unknown,
For the old ages with gold in heart?

Do you not hear the sighing of a reed in Japan,
(In Japan beyond, in Japan beyond)
In the voice of a bird who long ago flew away,
For the old peace with velvet-sandalled feet?

CRADLE SONGS

I

Sleep, my love, your way of dream
By the fireflies shall be lighted,
That I gather from the heart of night.
Your father is off, good night,
To buy the honey from the stars:
The city of stars is away a hundred miles.
But by the dawn he will return,
Riding on the horse of the dews,
For you, with a drum as big as the sun.

II

The flowers are nodding
Above your head;
The flowers are made with sorrows seven,
And laughters three which are the best.

The sorrows seven your mother keeps,
(Mother's way is that of pain,)
But the laughters three make you fair and gay,
I rock you, fairy boat on the tide of love.

Sleep, my own, till the bell of dusk
Bring the stars laden with a dream;
With that dream you shall awake
Between the laughters and song.

FROM "JAPANESE HOKKUS" (1920)

Japanese Hokkus

I

What is life? A voice,
A thought, a light on the dark,—
Lo, crow in the sky.

II

Sudden pain of earth
I hear in the fallen leaf.
"Life's autumn," I cry.

III

The silence-leaves from Life,
Older than dream or pain,—
Are they my passing ghost?

IV

Is it not the cry of a rose to be saved?
Oh, how could I
When I, in fact, am the rose!

V

But the march to Life. . .
Break song to sing the new song!
Clouds leap, flowers bloom.

VI

Fallen leaves! Nay, spirits?
Shall I go downward with thee
By a stream of Fate?

VII

Speak not again, Voice!
The silence washes off sins:
Come not again, Light!

VIII

It is too late to hear a nightingale?
Tut, tut, tut, . . . some bird sings,—
That's quite enough, my friend.

IX

I shall cry to thee across the years?
Wilt thou turn thy face to respond
To my own tears with thy smile?

X

Where the flowers sleep,
Thank God! I shall sleep, to-night.
Oh, come, butterfly!

XI

My Love's lengthened hair
Swings o'er me from Heaven's gate:
Lo, Evening's shadow!

XII

Is there anything new under the sun?
Certainly there is.
See how a bird flies, how flowers smile!

Yone Noguchi (1875–1947) was a Japanese poet, novelist, and critic who wrote in both English and Japanese. Born in Tsushima, he studied the works of Thomas Carlyle and Herbert Spencer at Keio University in Tokyo, where he also practiced Zen and wrote haiku. In 1893, he moved to San Francisco and began working at a newspaper established by Japanese exiles. Under the tutelage of Joaquin Miller, an Oakland-based writer and outdoorsman, Noguchi came into his own as a poet. He published two collections in 1897 before moving to New York via Chicago. In 1901, he published *The American Diary of a Japanese Girl*, his debut novel. Noguchi soon tired of America, however, and sailed to England where he published a third book of poems and made connections with such writers as William Butler Yeats and Thomas Hardy. Reinvigorated and determined to continue his career, he returned to New York in 1903, but left for Japan the following year following the end of his marriage to journalist and educator Léonie Gilmour, with whom he had a son. As the Russo-Japanese War brought his nation onto the world stage, Noguchi became known as a literary critic for the *Japan Times* and focused on advising such Western playwrights as Yeats to study the classical Noh drama. He spent the second decade of the century as a prominent international lecturer, mainly in Europe and Britain. In 1920, Noguchi published *Japanese Hokkus*, a collection of short poems, before turning his attention to Japanese-language verse. As Japan moved closer toward war with the West, Noguchi turned from leftist politics to the nationalism supported by his country's leaders, straining his relationship with Bengali poet Rabindranath Tagore and distancing himself from his former colleagues around the world. In 1945, his home in Tokyo was destroyed in the devastating American firebombing of the city; he died only two years later, having reconnected with his son Isamu.

A Note from the Publisher

Spanning many genres, from non-fiction essays to literature classics to children's books and lyric poetry, Mint Edition books showcase the master works of our time in a modern new package. The text is freshly typeset, is clean and easy to read, and features a new note about the author in each volume. Many books also include exclusive new introductory material. Every book boasts a striking new cover, which makes it as appropriate for collecting as it is for gift giving. Mint Edition books are only printed when a reader orders them, so natural resources are not wasted. We're proud that our books are never manufactured in excess and exist only in the exact quantity they need to be read and enjoyed.

bookfinity™

Discover more of your favorite classics with Bookfinity™.

- Track your reading with custom book lists.
- Get great book recommendations for your personalized Reader Type.
- Add reviews for your favorite books.
- AND MUCH MORE!

Visit **bookfinity.com** and take the fun Reader Type quiz to get started.

Enjoy our classic and modern companion pairings!

Classic & Modern